CATS' WHISPERS

CATS' WHISPERS

The cream of cat cartoons

edited by S. Gross

COLUMBUS BOOKS
LONDON

Some of the cartoons in this collection have appeared in the following periodicals and are reprinted by permission of the authors: *Audubon, Better Homes and Gardens, Boys' Life, Campus Life, Cavalier, Cosmopolitan, Diversion, Family Circle, Good Housekeeping, Gourmet, House & Garden, Ladies' Home Journal, National Enquirer, National Lampoon, 1000 Jokes, Oui, Parade, Penthouse, Philadelphia Inquirer Magazine, Playboy, Punch, Saturday Evening Post, Saturday Review, This Week, TV Guide, Vision, Woman's Day, The Yacht.*

Grateful acknowledgment is made for permission to reprint:

Cartoon by George Booth on page 37 from *Playboy* Copyright © 1974 by Playboy. Reproduced by special permission of *Playboy* magazine.

Cartoons by Roz Chast from *Parallel Universes.* Copyright © 1984 by Roz Chast. Reproduced by permission of the author.

Cartoon by Samuel H. Gross on page 58 reprinted with permission from *TV Guide* magazine. Copyright © 1976 by Triangle Publications, Inc., Radnor, Pennsylvania.

Cartoons by Sidney Harris on pages 40 and 111 from *Playboy.* Copyright © 1971, 1979 by Playboy. Reproduced by special permission of *Playboy* magazine.

Cartoon by Henry Martin on page 95 from *Punch.* Copyright © 1979 by *Punch.* Reprinted by permission of Rothco Cartoons Inc. and the author.

Cartoons by John S. P. Walker. Reprinted from *Bad Dogs* by John S. P. Walker. Copyright © 1982 by John S. P. Walker. Reprinted by permission of Alfred A. Knopf. Inc. and Methuen and Company, Ltd.

Cartoons copyrighted by *The New Yorker* are indicated throughout the book.

Designer: Kim Llewellyn

First published in Great Britain in 1988 by
Columbus Books Limited
19-23 Ludgate Hill, London EC4M 7PD
Reprinted 1988

Published by arrangement with Harper & Row, Publishers, Inc., New York, New York, USA

Printed and bound by The Guernsey Press, Guernsey, CI

ISBN 0 86287 151 4

"So tell us—what is all this controversy *really* about?"

"Aw quit your bellyaching, you're the one who got drunk and brought the damn thing home."

BILL WOODMAN

JACK ZIEGLER

"I liked it, but I still don't like the real ones."

VAHAN
SHIRVANIAN

"Are you coming down or am I coming
up there?"

7

The Allergic Guest

8

"Everyone be home by two o'clock!"

S. GROSS

SAM GROSS

"Are you still feeding that alley cat?"

ORLANDO BUSINO

11

HOW TO DISPOSE OF A CAT

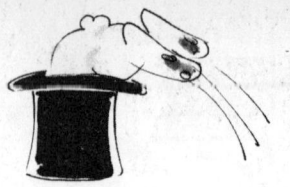

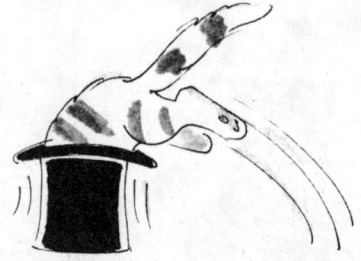

BERNARD SCHOENBAUM

ED FRASCINO

"Has one of you been nosing around
among my souvenirs again?"

BORIS DRUCKER

"Hi there, this is a cat food commercial. I'll wait
while you get your cat."

WOODMAN

HENRY MARTIN

"You may go out, but no concertizing."

ORLANDO BUSINO

"Her flea collar is too tight because you haven't changed it since she was a kitten."

"The fact that you cats were considered sacred in ancient Egypt cuts no ice with me."

J.B. HANDELSMAN

JACK ZIEGLER

DON OREHEK

18   "How was your day at the fish market, dear?"

JARED LEE

"You know what you need? You need
a backpack."

ED FISHER

"What I really can't stand is his 'more
familiar than thou' attitude."

19

MICHAEL MASLIN

© 1982 The New Yorker Magazine, Inc.

BILL MAUL

21

"Putty took a wife. Her name was Pussums, and she bore him Little Gentleman, Biddy Boo, Savor Tooth, Fluffy, Harry Cat, and Caesar. Then Little Gentleman begat Little Gentleman II and Friday and Twinkle Toes and Possum Tail and . . ."

BOOTH

GEORGE BOOTH

ED FRASCINO

"Would it kill you to try a little tenderness?"

MORT GERBERG

"What's the matter, dear? . . . . cat got your tongue?"

CHICKEN·ALERT

26

TIM HAGGERTY

"I'll have what she's having."

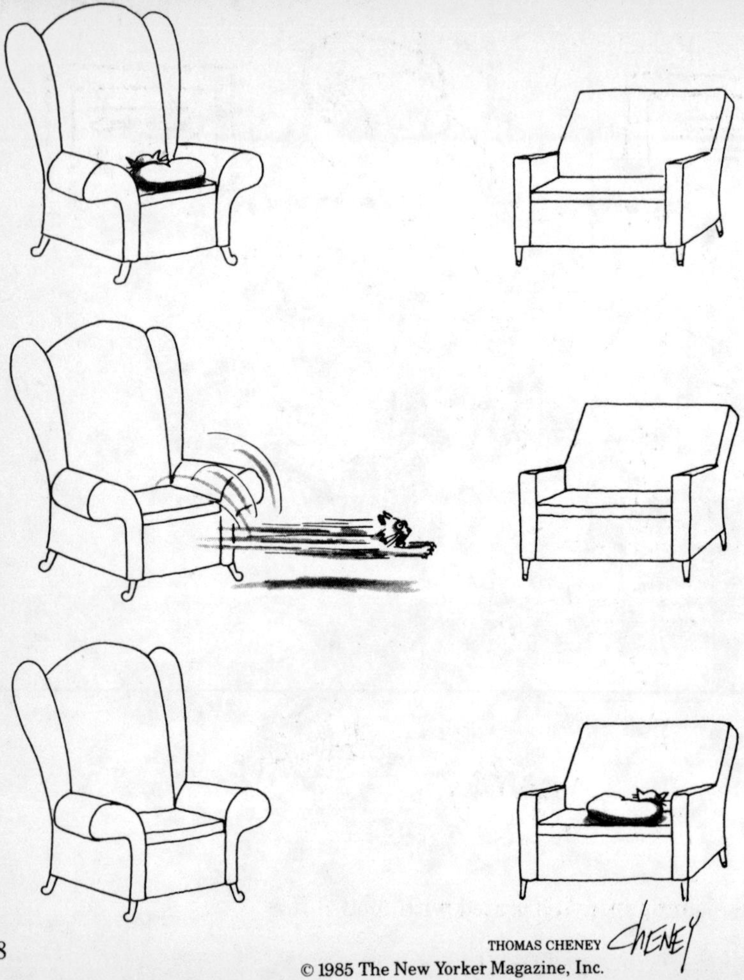

HENRY MARTIN

"Concerning my fancyleaf caladium, you have the right to remain silent and anything you say may be held against you."

THOMAS CHENEY

"No wonder her tongue doesn't feel like sandpaper. It's coated with mouse fur."

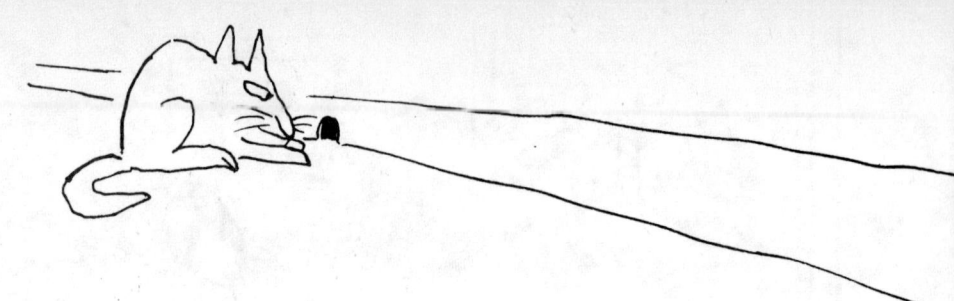

AL ROSS

S. GROSS

SAM GROSS

CHARLES SAXON
© 1985 The New Yorker Magazine, Inc.

"When she was little, we had a very close relationship,
but now we're just friends."

"It's ten o'clock. Do you know where your cat is?"

32

VAHAN SHIRVANIAN

WOODMAN

BILL WOODMAN

WILLIAM HOEST

"I realize you're lonely now that the children are gone, Helen, but . . . ."

"I'll see you to the door, Marsha . . . I want to be sure my cat doesn't slip out."

JO LINKERT

BERNARD SCHOENBAUM

"Where in the world have you been for the past three months?"

35

GUM for CATS

R. Chast

BOOTH
GEORGE BOOTH

"Let's take the Andantino in C again . . . this time without the cat!"

"Am I talking to *myself?*"

39

SIDNEY HARRIS

"My advice is keep away from it. You start with catnip, and before you know it,
you're on heroin."

"I don't know. Maybe she picked it up from watching figure skaters on the TV."

TIM HAGGERTY

MORT GERBERG

42

"I'm sorry. I should have warned you. We have bad cat karma."

JOHN JONIK

HENRY MARTIN

". . . and I don't want to find this place in a
shambles when we get back."

43

TIME
3:05

TEMP
68°

CATS
53 ZILLION

AARON BACALL

"All right, come out and we'll talk about it."

44

FRANK MODELL

"It would appear we're in someone's litterbox."

BILL MAUL

45

"She bumps into things."

JOHN NORMENT

DON OREHEK

48

"You're getting him fixed? I didn't know he was broken."

PUSS 'N CLOGS

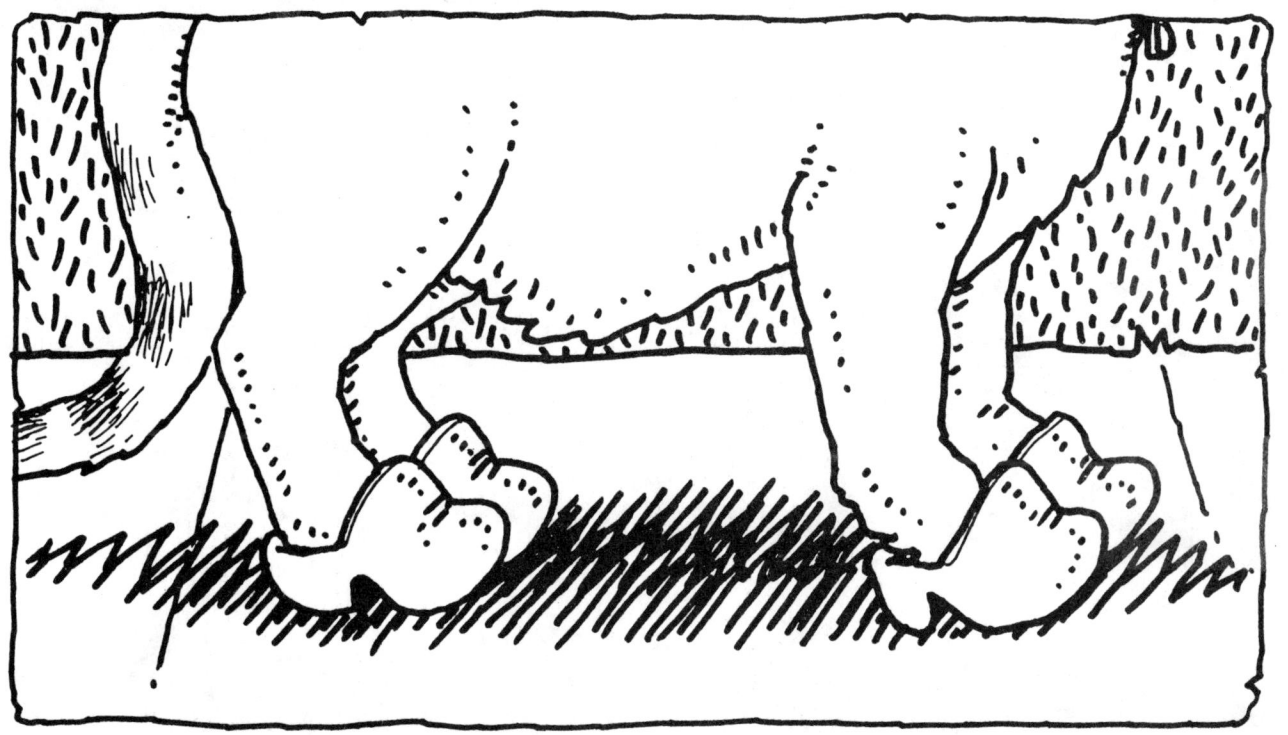

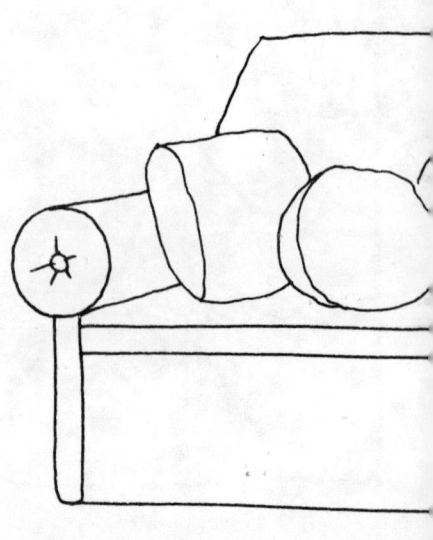

50   "You may have nine lives but remember they're concurrent."

CHENEY

THOMAS CHENEY

"It's worked out well, actually. They're cat
people and I'm, as it turns out, a people cat."

JACK ZIEGLER

JOSEPH FARRIS

ORLANDO BUSINO

"Grace and I have always considered you a friend, Delbert . . . a real friend . . . I mean a *real* friend. . . ."

BILL WOODMAN   WOODMAN

"Then as the coup de grâce she turned my own cat against me."

ED FRASCINO

"Thank goodness, you remembered the cat food!"

CATHARINE O'NEILL

56

JOHN S.P. WALKER

Man Caught in the Act of Cat-Hurling

SIDNEY HARRIS

"They get along beautifully. The dog thinks he's
a cat and the cat thinks she's a dog."

"Nothing to worry about, folks, I'm just going
to let the cat in."

DON OREHEK

S.GROSS

SAM GROSS

58

"I'm going to give away all the cats and cancel my magazine subscriptions, and then I'm going to paint ten pickets a day!"

"She used to purr more often before she got spayed."

CATHERINE SIRACUSA

"I may not know anything about art, but I do know what I hate."

PAUL and WILLIE'S SHOE STORE, BEING ATTACKED BY CATS.

BILL WOODMAN

62

VAHAN SHIRVANIAN

63

65

1

2

3

4

5

6

7

ARNOLDO FRANCHIONI

TOO CUTE FOR COMFORT

ROZ CHAST
© 1980 The New Yorker Magazine, Inc.

MICK STEVENS

The Last Robin of Spring

"I'm letting her have one last fling. She's getting declawed tomorrow."

BERNARD SCHOENBAUM

69

"Have you been filling his head with lies about me again?"

· ED FRASCINO

AARON BACALL

"Turn around and look cute and adorable!"

JOHN CASSADY

"This year I'm giving all those I care
for dead birds."

HENRY MARTIN

"Muffy, where are you?"

SIDNEY HARRIS

"My favorite is the Late Show. By that time
the set is nice and warm."

O'NEILL
CATHARINE O'NEILL

"You've waited twenty-eight years to tell me,
Marcia? You're a dog person?!"

73

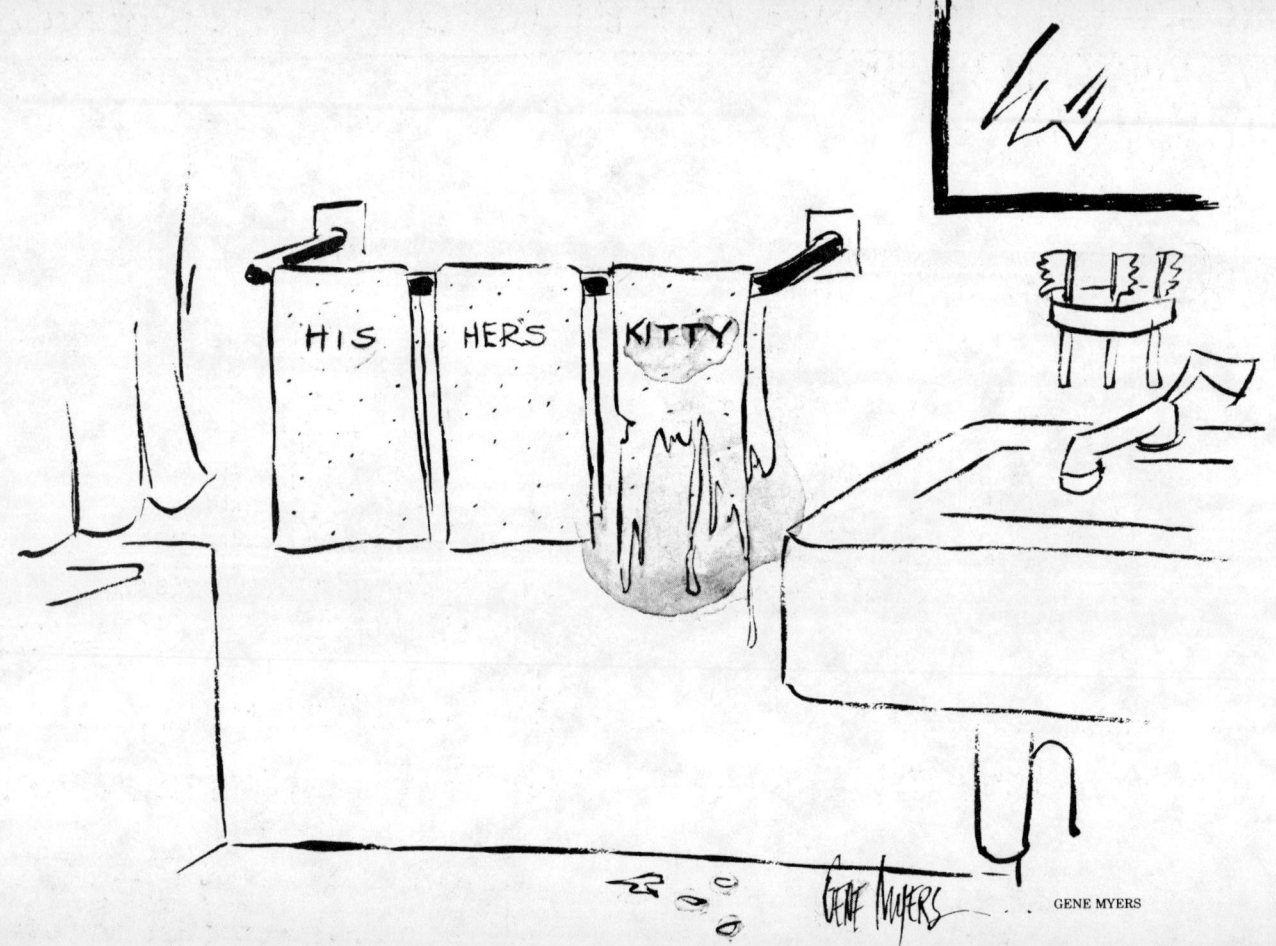

GENE MYERS

TACKY CAT HAVING A RELIGIOUS EXPERIENCE

...IN A NEW OIL SPOT ON THE DRIVEWAY.

OLIVER CHRISTIANSON (REVILO)

BERNARD SCHOENBAUM

"Edgar, the cat wants in. And I want *out*."

MORT GERBERG

"Oh, no you don't, Mrs. Grumfeld! You don't get rid of them *that* easily!"

BILL MAUL

79

"You have to admit that the kitty was adorable, even
if you can't stand cat-food commercials."

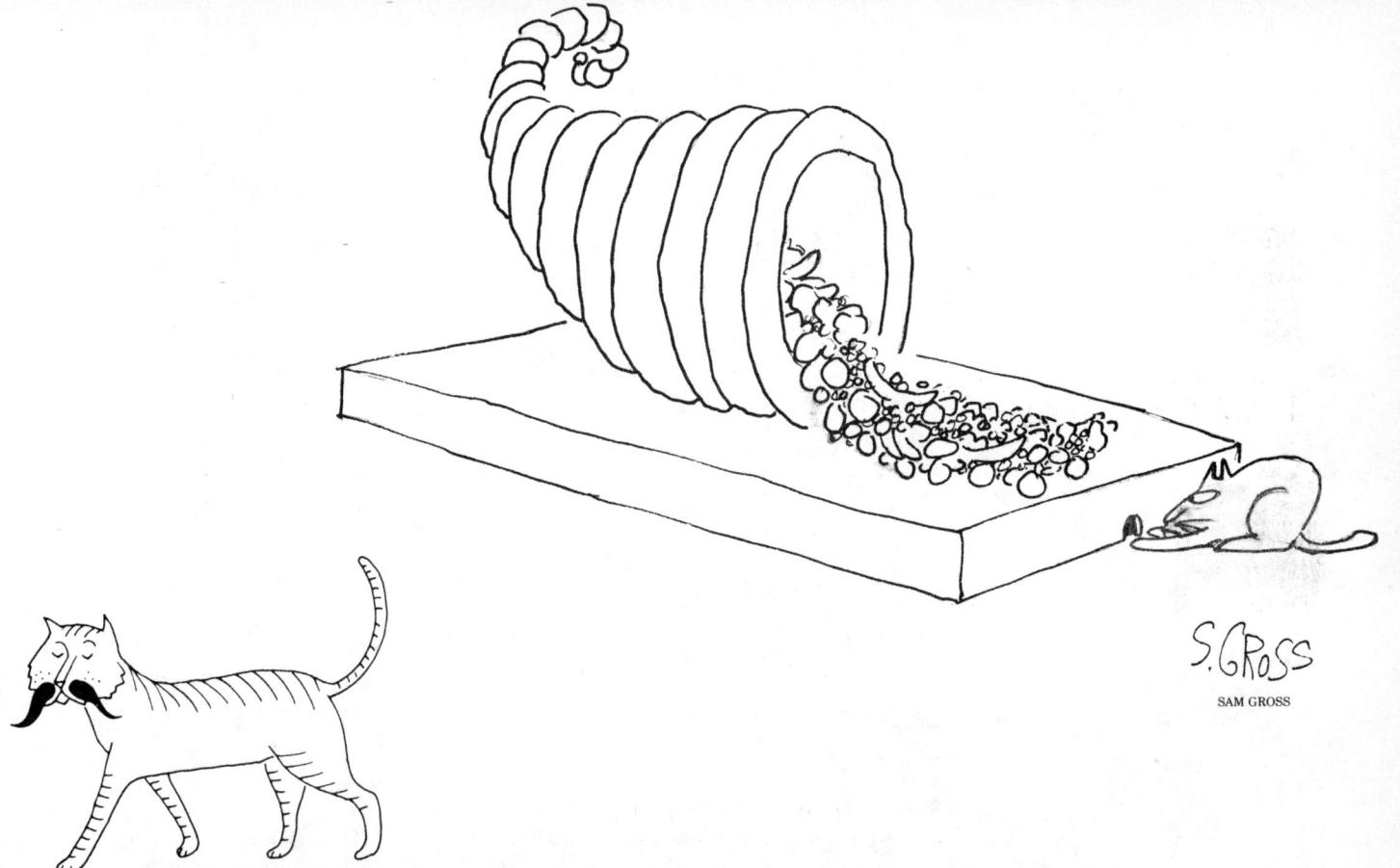

S.GROSS
SAM GROSS

feggo FELIPE GALINDO (FEGGO)

81

"She *looks* innocent enough, but she's had twenty-nine kids."

Baloo

DON OREHEK

"Actually it's quite reasonable when you consider you're buying nine lives."

83

MOVIES FOR CATS

Fluffy Gets Fed

Yarn

Of Mice and Birds

R. Chast

"He looks so wistful, let's get him a companion."

DAVID SIPRESS

AL ROSS

GAHAN WILSON

"Just what do you think *you're* up to?"

85

"Kitty's upset."

P.C. VEY

BERNARD SCHOENBAUM

"Eat it or you won't get any dessert."

VAHAN SHIRVANIAN

"A cat that fetches things. How about *that*? A cat that fetches. I'll be damned."

WARREN MILLER

TIM HAGGERTY

BORIS DRUCKER

"Does he have to keep rubbing his whiskers on the floor?"

"Sure I know their names. . . . She's
Pretty Kitty and he's Damn Cat."

ANDY WYATT

LEO CULLUM

"I've always felt cats were sort of sneaky—"

MICHAEL MASLIN

An Inside Job

"I have something in common with Queen Elizabeth. We both have animal hair on the furniture. Hers is corgi; mine is cat."

GEORGE BOOTH

HENRY MARTIN

"You know what I like about you? You
don't talk, talk, talk, talk, talk, talk, talk."

ED FRASCINO

"She has hiccups. Can you sneak up and
scare her?"

"I told you not to call him 'pussycat'!"

"Cat Yummies *again?*"

WOODMAN

BILL WOODMAN

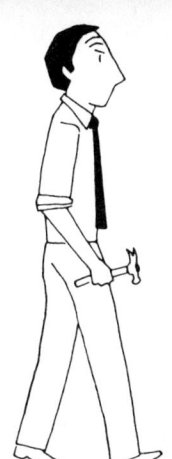

FELIPE GALINDO (FEGGO)

ED FRASCINO

"You're a good listener, Ralph."

Cheshire Cat Revisited

CHARLES SAUE

"Bye-bye, have a mice day."

MICHAEL MASLIN

"I tried to make it from the windowsill to the top of the refrigerator. How about you?"

THOMAS CHENEY
© 1985 The New Yorker Magazine, Inc.

TONY ROSA

GEORGE BOOTH

"Today has been difficult, Lucille. Wellington foozled his drive at the
ninth tee, and the people next door adopted a new pale-fawn Siamese cat."

"Would you let the cat out again, Frank?"

BILL MAUL

"Did you tell the cat he could have some of these licorice strings?"

CAT'S PAJAMAS

ROZ CHAST R. Chast

BOOTH

GEORGE BOO

"Boss? I've sprung a leak."

"Andy and I split. He came home one day with *two* Irish wolfhounds."

BARNEY TOBEY

VAHAN SHIRVANIAN

BERNARD SCHOENBAUM

"Alphonse. You're a bum!"

SIDNEY HARRIS

"If you don't have a beeper, then you're sitting on my cat."

"We can't afford her full time. We share her with the people across the hall."

ED FRASCINO

BILL MAUL

"See? Thunder and lightning is God's
way of saying, 'Buffy Barnes, don't
be such a picky eater!' . . ."

MICHAEL CRAWFORD

After Mary Cassatt: Girl Arranging Her Cat

HENRY MARTIN

"We'll miss you, but I can't promise we won't talk about you when you're gone."

S.GROSS

SAM GROSS

BERNARD SCHOENBAUM

"Lord, what a day! On top of everything else, the cat passed away."

"Gato!"

CHARLES SAUERS

"Careful. She has an unpredictable sense of humor."

ED FRASCINO

CAT AEROBICS

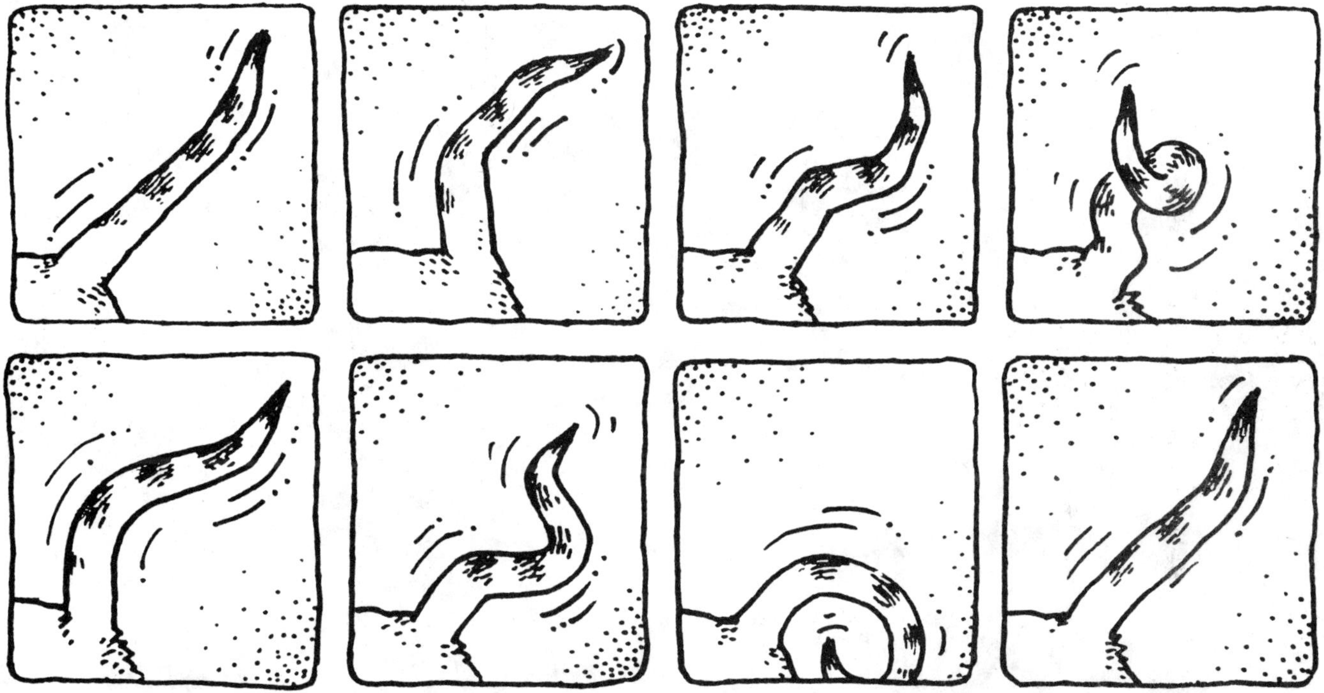

OLIVER CHRISTIANSON (REVILO)

119

"Meow!"   "Meow!"   "Meow, godammit!"

BORIS DRUCKER

MIXED BREED

CALICO

MALTESE

MANX

ANGORA

PERSIAN

SIAMESE

Stuart Leeds
STUART LEEDS

"Hey Dummy! Who gave you that bell?"

PCVEY
P.C. VEY

"Friday the 15th. Dear diary, in an effort to keep up with the times I have laid aside my pen and taken up the microphone. Pussy-cat is having a field day with the cord, leaping here and there. . . ."

H. Martin

HENRY MARTIN

"I'll bet it's been years since a crumb fell all the way to the floor."

SEEING EYE CAT TRAINING SCHOOL

THOMAS CHENEY

"Darling, I told you male cats have a tendency to spray."

JOHN CALLAHAN

PETER PORGES

"Now do you believe me that your hair tonic smells like tunafish?"

"Must you wear your campaign ribbons in here?"

ED FRASCINO

feggo

FELIPE GALINDO (FEGGO)